Dieses Buch gehört

WOCHENPLANER

Montag

Dienstag

Mittwoch

Donnerstag

Freitag

Dringende To Dos:

*
*
*
*
*

Andere To-Dos:

*
*
*
*
*
*
*
*
*
*
*
*
*
*
*

Freundlichkeit der Woche:

Gesund gelebt?

	M	D	M	D	F	S	S

WOCHENPLANER

Woche:

Montag

Dienstag

Mittwoch

Donnerstag

Freitag

Dringende To Dos:

* ____________________
* ____________________
* ____________________
* ____________________
* ____________________

Andere To Dos:

* ____________________
* ____________________
* ____________________
* ____________________
* ____________________
* ____________________
* ____________________
* ____________________
* ____________________
* ____________________
* ____________________
* ____________________
* ____________________
* ____________________
* ____________________
* ____________________

Freundlichkeit der Woche:

Gesund gelebt?   M D M D F S S

	M	D	M	D	F	S	S

WOCHENPLANER

Montag

Dienstag

Mittwoch

Donnerstag

Freitag

Dringende To Dos:

* ______________
* ______________
* ______________
* ______________
* ______________

Andere To Dos:

* ______________
* ______________
* ______________
* ______________
* ______________
* ______________
* ______________
* ______________
* ______________
* ______________
* ______________
* ______________
* ______________
* ______________
* ______________

Freundlichkeit der Woche:

Gesund gelebt?

	M	D	M	D	F	S	S

WOCHENPLANER

Woche:

Montag

Dienstag

Mittwoch

Donnerstag

Freitag

Dringende To Dos:

*
*
*
*
*

Andere To Dos:

*
*
*
*
*
*
*
*
*
*
*
*
*
*

Freundlichkeit der Woche:

Gesund gelebt? M D M D F S S

WOCHENPLANER

Montag

Dienstag

Mittwoch

Donnerstag

Freitag

Dringende To Dos:

* --
* --
* --
* --
* --

Andere To Dos:

* --
* --
* --
* --
* --
* --
* --
* --
* --
* --
* --
* --
* --
* --
* --

Freundlichkeit der Woche:

Gesund gelebt?   M   D   M   D   F   S   S

	M	D	M	D	F	S	S

WOCHENPLANER

Montag

Dienstag

Mittwoch

Donnerstag

Freitag

Dringende To Dos:

* ....
* ....
* ....
* ....
* ....

Andere To Dos:

* ....
* ....
* ....
* ....
* ....
* ....
* ....
* ....
* ....
* ....
* ....
* ....
* ....
* ....
* ....
* ....
* ....

Freundlichkeit der Woche:

Gesund gelebt?	M	D	M	D	F	S	S

WOCHENPLANER

Montag

Dienstag

Mittwoch

Donnerstag

Freitag

Dringende To-Dos:

*
*
*
*
*

Andere To-Dos:

*
*
*
*
*
*
*
*
*
*
*
*
*
*
*

Freundlichkeit der Woche:

Gesund gelebt?   M D M D F S S

WOCHENPLANER

Montag

Dienstag

Mittwoch

Donnerstag

Freitag

WEEKEND

Dringende To Dos:

*
*
*
*
*

Andere To-Dos:

*
*
*
*
*
*
*
*
*
*
*
*
*
*
*

Freundlichkeit der Woche:

Gesund gelebt?   M D M D F S S

	M	D	M	D	F	S	S

WOCHENPLANER

Montag

Dienstag

Mittwoch

Donnerstag

Freitag

Dringende To Dos:

*
*
*
*
*

Andere To Dos:

*
*
*
*
*
*
*
*
*
*
*
*
*
*
*

Freundlichkeit der Woche:

Gesund gelebt?	M	D	M	D	F	S	S

WOCHENPLANER

Montag

Dienstag

Mittwoch

Donnerstag

Freitag

Dringende To Dos:

* ....
* ....
* ....
* ....
* ....

Andere To-Dos:

* ....
* ....
* ....
* ....
* ....
* ....
* ....
* ....
* ....
* ....
* ....
* ....
* ....
* ....
* ....

Freundlichkeit der Woche:

Gesund gelebt?

	M	D	M	D	F	S	S

WOCHENPLANER

Montag

Dienstag

Mittwoch

Donnerstag

Freitag

Dringende To Dos:

* ....
* ....
* ....
* ....
* ....

Andere To Dos:

* ....
* ....
* ....
* ....
* ....
* ....
* ....
* ....
* ....
* ....
* ....
* ....
* ....
* ....
* ....

Freundlichkeit der Woche:

Gesund gelebt? M D M D F S S

WOCHENPLANER

Montag

Dienstag

Mittwoch

Donnerstag

Freitag

Dringende To Dos:

*
*
*
*
*

Andere To Dos:

*
*
*
*
*
*
*
*
*
*
*
*
*
*
*

Freundlichkeit der Woche:

Gesund gelebt?   M   D   M   D   F   S   S

WOCHENPLANER

Montag

Dienstag

Mittwoch

Donnerstag

Freitag

Dringende To Dos:

*
*
*
*
*

Andere To Dos:

*
*
*
*
*
*
*
*
*
*
*
*
*
*
*

Freundlichkeit der Woche:

Gesund gelebt?

	M	D	M	D	F	S	S

WOCHENPLANER

Woche:

Montag

Dienstag

Mittwoch

Donnerstag

Freitag

WEEKEND

Dringende To Dos:

* --------------------------------
* --------------------------------
* --------------------------------
* --------------------------------
* --------------------------------

Andere To Dos:

* --------------------------------
* --------------------------------
* --------------------------------
* --------------------------------
* --------------------------------
* --------------------------------
* --------------------------------
* --------------------------------
* --------------------------------
* --------------------------------
* --------------------------------
* --------------------------------
* --------------------------------
* --------------------------------
* --------------------------------

Freundlichkeit der Woche:

Gesund gelebt?	M	D	M	D	F	S	S

WOCHENPLANER

Montag

Dienstag

Mittwoch

Donnerstag

Freitag

Dringende To Dos:

*
*
*
*
*

Andere To Dos:

*
*
*
*
*
*
*
*
*
*
*
*
*
*
*

Freundlichkeit der Woche:

Gesund gelebt? M D M D F S S

WOCHENPLANER

Montag

Dienstag

Mittwoch

Donnerstag

Freitag

Dringende To Dos:

* ....
* ....
* ....
* ....
* ....

Andere To-Dos:

* ....
* ....
* ....
* ....
* ....
* ....
* ....
* ....
* ....
* ....
* ....
* ....
* ....
* ....
* ....

Freundlichkeit der Woche:

Gesund gelebt?

	M	D	M	D	F	S	S

WOCHENPLANER

Montag

Dienstag

Mittwoch

Donnerstag

Freitag

Dringende To Dos:

*
*
*
*
*

Andere To Dos:

*
*
*
*
*
*
*
*
*
*
*
*
*
*

Freundlichkeit der Woche:

Gesund gelebt? M D M D F S S

WOCHENPLANER

Montag

Dienstag

Mittwoch

Donnerstag

Freitag

Dringende To Dos:

*
*
*
*
*

Andere To Dos:

*
*
*
*
*
*
*
*
*
*
*
*
*
*
*

Freundlichkeit der Woche:

Gesund gelebt?	M	D	M	D	F	S	S

WOCHENPLANER

Montag

Dienstag

Mittwoch

Donnerstag

Freitag

Dringende To-Dos:

*
*
*
*
*

Andere To-Dos:

*
*
*
*
*
*
*
*
*
*
*
*
*
*

Freundlichkeit der Woche:

Gesund gelebt? M D M D F S S

WOCHENPLANER

Montag

Dienstag

Mittwoch

Donnerstag

Freitag

Dringende To Dos:

*
*
*
*
*

Andere To Dos:

*
*
*
*
*
*
*
*
*
*
*
*
*
*
*

Freundlichkeit der Woche:

Gesund gelebt?   M D M D F S S

WOCHENPLANER

Montag

Dienstag

Mittwoch

Donnerstag

Freitag

Dringende To Dos:

* ______________________________
* ______________________________
* ______________________________
* ______________________________
* ______________________________

Andere To Dos:

* ______________________________
* ______________________________
* ______________________________
* ______________________________
* ______________________________
* ______________________________
* ______________________________
* ______________________________
* ______________________________
* ______________________________
* ______________________________
* ______________________________
* ______________________________
* ______________________________
* ______________________________
* ______________________________

Freundlichkeit der Woche:

Gesund gelebt?   M D M D F S S

WOCHENPLANER

Montag

Dienstag

Mittwoch

Donnerstag

Freitag

Dringende To Dos:

* ....
* ....
* ....
* ....
* ....

Andere To Dos:

* ....
* ....
* ....
* ....
* ....
* ....
* ....
* ....
* ....
* ....
* ....
* ....
* ....
* ....
* ....
* ....
* ....

Freundlichkeit der Woche:

Gesund gelebt? M D M D F S S

WOCHENPLANER

Montag

Dienstag

Mittwoch

Donnerstag

Freitag

Dringende To Dos:

*..
*..
*..
*..
*..

Andere To Dos:

*..
*..
*..
*..
*..
*..
*..
*..
*..
*..
*..
*..
*..
*..

Freundlichkeit der Woche:

Gesund gelebt? M D M D F S S

WOCHENPLANER

Woche:

Montag

Dienstag

Mittwoch

Donnerstag

Freitag

WEEKEND

Dringende To Dos:

*
*
*
*
*

Andere To Dos:

*
*
*
*
*
*
*
*
*
*
*
*
*
*

Freundlichkeit der Woche:

Gesund gelebt? M D M D F S S

WOCHENPLANER

Montag

Dienstag

Mittwoch

Donnerstag

Freitag

Dringende To Dos:

*
*
*
*
*

Andere To Dos:

*
*
*
*
*
*
*
*
*
*
*
*
*
*

Freundlichkeit der Woche:

Gesund gelebt? M D M D F S S

WOCHENPLANER

Montag

Dienstag

Mittwoch

Donnerstag

Freitag

Dringende To Dos:

*
*
*
*
*

Andere To-Dos:

*
*
*
*
*
*
*
*
*
*
*
*
*
*

Freundlichkeit der Woche:

Gesund gelebt?	M	D	M	D	F	S	S

WOCHENPLANER

Woche:

Montag

Dienstag

Mittwoch

Donnerstag

Freitag

Dringende To Dos:

*
*
*
*
*

Andere To Dos:

*
*
*
*
*
*
*
*
*
*
*
*
*
*

Freundlichkeit der Woche:

Gesund gelebt?	M	D	M	D	F	S	S

WOCHENPLANER

Montag

Dienstag

Mittwoch

Donnerstag

Freitag

Dringende To Dos:

*
*
*
*
*

Andere To Dos:

*
*
*
*
*
*
*
*
*
*
*
*
*
*
*

Freundlichkeit der Woche:

Gesund gelebt?   M   D   M   D   F   S   S

WOCHENPLANER

Montag

Dienstag

Mittwoch

Donnerstag

Freitag

Dringende To Dos:

* _______________________________
* _______________________________
* _______________________________
* _______________________________
* _______________________________

Andere To Dos:

* _______________________________
* _______________________________
* _______________________________
* _______________________________
* _______________________________
* _______________________________
* _______________________________
* _______________________________
* _______________________________
* _______________________________
* _______________________________
* _______________________________
* _______________________________
* _______________________________
* _______________________________

Freundlichkeit der Woche:

Gesund gelebt?   M D M D F S S

WOCHENPLANER

Woche:

Montag

Dienstag

Mittwoch

Donnerstag

Freitag

Dringende To Dos:

*
*
*
*
*

Andere To Dos:

*
*
*
*
*
*
*
*
*
*
*
*
*
*
*

Freundlichkeit der Woche:

Gesund gelebt?	M	D	M	D	F	S	S

WOCHENPLANER

Montag

Dienstag

Mittwoch

Donnerstag

Freitag

Dringende To Dos:

* ....
* ....
* ....
* ....
* ....

Andere To Dos:

* ....
* ....
* ....
* ....
* ....
* ....
* ....
* ....
* ....
* ....
* ....
* ....
* ....
* ....
* ....
* ....

Freundlichkeit der Woche:

Gesund gelebt?

Gesund gelebt?	M	D	M	D	F	S	S

WOCHENPLANER

Woche:

Montag

Dienstag

Mittwoch

Donnerstag

Freitag

Dringende To Dos:

*
*
*
*
*

Andere To Dos:

*
*
*
*
*
*
*
*
*
*
*
*
*
*

Freundlichkeit der Woche:

Gesund gelebt?

	M	D	M	D	F	S	S

WOCHENPLANER

Montag

Dienstag

Mittwoch

Donnerstag

Freitag

Dringende To Dos:

*
*
*
*
*

Andere To Dos:

*
*
*
*
*
*
*
*
*
*
*
*
*
*
*

Freundlichkeit der Woche:

Gesund gelebt? M D M D F S S

WOCHENPLANER

Montag

Dienstag

Mittwoch

Donnerstag

Freitag

Dringende To Dos:

*
*
*
*
*

Andere To-Dos:

*
*
*
*
*
*
*
*
*
*
*
*
*
*
*

Freundlichkeit der Woche:

Gesund gelebt?	M	D	M	D	F	S	S

WOCHENPLANER

Woche:

Montag

Dienstag

Mittwoch

Donnerstag

Freitag

WEEKEND

Dringende To Dos:

*
*
*
*
*

Andere To Dos:

*
*
*
*
*
*
*
*
*
*
*
*
*
*
*

Freundlichkeit der Woche:

Gesund gelebt?	M	D	M	D	F	S	S

WOCHENPLANER

Woche:

Montag

Dienstag

Mittwoch

Donnerstag

Freitag

Dringende To Dos:

*
*
*
*
*

Andere To Dos:

*
*
*
*
*
*
*
*
*
*
*
*
*
*
*

Freundlichkeit der Woche:

Gesund gelebt?

	M	D	M	D	F	S	S

WOCHENPLANER

Woche:

Montag

Dienstag

Mittwoch

Donnerstag

Freitag

WEEKEND

Dringende To Dos:

* ________________
* ________________
* ________________
* ________________
* ________________

Andere To-Dos:

* ________________
* ________________
* ________________
* ________________
* ________________
* ________________
* ________________
* ________________
* ________________
* ________________
* ________________
* ________________
* ________________
* ________________

Freundlichkeit der Woche:

Gesund gelebt?

	M	D	M	D	F	S	S

WOCHENPLANER

Montag

Dienstag

Mittwoch

Donnerstag

Freitag

Dringende To Dos:

*
*
*
*
*

Andere To-Dos:

*
*
*
*
*
*
*
*
*
*
*
*
*
*
*

Freundlichkeit der Woche:

Gesund gelebt?

	M	D	M	D	F	S	S

WOCHENPLANER

Montag

Dienstag

Mittwoch

Donnerstag

Freitag

Dringende To Dos:

* ....
* ....
* ....
* ....
* ....

Andere To Dos:

* ....
* ....
* ....
* ....
* ....
* ....
* ....
* ....
* ....
* ....
* ....
* ....
* ....
* ....
* ....

Freundlichkeit der Woche:

Gesund gelebt?

	M	D	M	D	F	S	S

WOCHENPLANER

Woche:

Montag

Dienstag

Mittwoch

Donnerstag

Freitag

Dringende To Dos:

* ....
* ....
* ....
* ....
* ....

Andere To Dos:

* ....
* ....
* ....
* ....
* ....
* ....
* ....
* ....
* ....
* ....
* ....
* ....
* ....
* ....

Freundlichkeit der Woche:

Gesund gelebt?

	M	D	M	D	F	S	S

WOCHENPLANER

Woche:

Montag

Dienstag

Mittwoch

Donnerstag

Freitag

Dringende To Dos:

*
*
*
*
*

Andere To Dos:

*
*
*
*
*
*
*
*
*
*
*
*
*
*

Freundlichkeit der Woche:

Gesund gelebt?

	M	D	M	D	F	S	S

WOCHENPLANER

Montag

Dienstag

Mittwoch

Donnerstag

Freitag

Dringende To Dos:

*
*
*
*
*

Andere To Dos:

*
*
*
*
*
*
*
*
*
*
*
*
*
*

Freundlichkeit der Woche:

Gesund gelebt?

	M	D	M	D	F	S	S

WOCHENPLANER

Montag

Dienstag

Mittwoch

Donnerstag

Freitag

Dringende To Dos:

*
*
*
*
*

Andere To Dos:

*
*
*
*
*
*
*
*
*
*
*
*
*
*

Freundlichkeit der Woche:

Gesund gelebt?

	M	D	M	D	F	S	S

WOCHENPLANER

Montag

Dienstag

Mittwoch

Donnerstag

Freitag

Dringende To Dos:

* ....
* ....
* ....
* ....
* ....

Andere To Dos:

* ....
* ....
* ....
* ....
* ....
* ....
* ....
* ....
* ....
* ....
* ....
* ....
* ....
* ....
* ....

Freundlichkeit der Woche:

Gesund gelebt?

	M	D	M	D	F	S	S

WOCHENPLANER

Montag

Dienstag

Mittwoch

Donnerstag

Freitag

Dringende To Dos:

*
*
*
*
*

Andere To Dos:

*
*
*
*
*
*
*
*
*
*
*
*
*
*

Freundlichkeit der Woche:

Gesund gelebt? M D M D F S S

WOCHENPLANER

Montag

Dienstag

Mittwoch

Donnerstag

Freitag

Dringende To Dos:

*
*
*
*
*

Andere To-Dos:

*
*
*
*
*
*
*
*
*
*
*
*
*
*
*
*

Freundlichkeit der Woche:

Gesund gelebt?	M	D	M	D	F	S	S

WOCHENPLANER

Woche:

Montag

Dienstag

Mittwoch

Donnerstag

Freitag

WEEKEND

Dringende To Dos:

*
*
*
*
*

Andere To Dos:

*
*
*
*
*
*
*
*
*
*
*
*
*
*

Freundlichkeit der Woche:

Gesund gelebt? M D M D F S S

WOCHENPLANER

Montag

Dienstag

Mittwoch

Donnerstag

Freitag

Dringende To Dos:

* ___________________________
* ___________________________
* ___________________________
* ___________________________
* ___________________________

Andere To Dos:

* ___________________________
* ___________________________
* ___________________________
* ___________________________
* ___________________________
* ___________________________
* ___________________________
* ___________________________
* ___________________________
* ___________________________
* ___________________________
* ___________________________
* ___________________________
* ___________________________

Freundlichkeit der Woche:

Gesund gelebt?   M D M D F S S

WOCHENPLANER

Montag

Dienstag

Mittwoch

Donnerstag

Freitag

Dringende To Dos:

*
*
*
*
*

Andere To Dos:

*
*
*
*
*
*
*
*
*
*
*
*
*
*

Freundlichkeit der Woche:

Gesund gelebt?

	M	D	M	D	F	S	S

WOCHENPLANER

Montag

Dienstag

Mittwoch

Donnerstag

Freitag

Dringende To Dos:

*
*
*
*
*

Andere To Dos:

*
*
*
*
*
*
*
*
*
*
*
*
*
*
*

Freundlichkeit der Woche:

Gesund gelebt?

	M	D	M	D	F	S	S

WOCHENPLANER

Montag

Dienstag

Mittwoch

Donnerstag

Freitag

WEEKEND

Dringende To Dos:

* ....
* ....
* ....
* ....
* ....

Andere To Dos:

* ....
* ....
* ....
* ....
* ....
* ....
* ....
* ....
* ....
* ....
* ....
* ....
* ....
* ....
* ....

Freundlichkeit der Woche:

Gesund gelebt? M D M D F S S

WOCHENPLANER

Montag

Dienstag

Mittwoch

Donnerstag

Freitag

Dringende To Dos:

* ....
* ....
* ....
* ....
* ....

Andere To Dos:

* ....
* ....
* ....
* ....
* ....
* ....
* ....
* ....
* ....
* ....
* ....
* ....
* ....
* ....
* ....

Freundlichkeit der Woche:

Gesund gelebt?

	M	D	M	D	F	S	S

WOCHENPLANER

Montag

Dienstag

Mittwoch

Donnerstag

Freitag

Dringende To Dos:

*
*
*
*
*

Andere To Dos:

*
*
*
*
*
*
*
*
*
*
*
*
*
*

Freundlichkeit der Woche:

Gesund gelebt? M D M D F S S

WOCHENPLANER

Woche:

Montag

Dienstag

Mittwoch

Donnerstag

Freitag

WEEKEND

Dringende To Dos:

*
*
*
*
*

Andere To Dos:

*
*
*
*
*
*
*
*
*
*
*
*
*
*
*

Freundlichkeit der Woche:

Gesund gelebt?

	M	D	M	D	F	S	S

WOCHENPLANER

Montag

Dienstag

Mittwoch

Donnerstag

Freitag

Dringende To Dos:

*
*
*
*
*

Andere To Dos:

*
*
*
*
*
*
*
*
*
*
*
*
*

Freundlichkeit der Woche:

Gesund gelebt?	M	D	M	D	F	S	S

WOCHENPLANER

Montag

Dienstag

Mittwoch

Donnerstag

Freitag

Dringende To Dos:

*
*
*
*
*

Andere To Dos:

*
*
*
*
*
*
*
*
*
*
*
*
*
*
*
*

Freundlichkeit der Woche:

Gesund gelebt?	M	D	M	D	F	S	S

WOCHENPLANER

Montag

Dienstag

Mittwoch

Donnerstag

Freitag

Dringende To Dos:

* ....
* ....
* ....
* ....
* ....

Andere To Dos:

* ....
* ....
* ....
* ....
* ....
* ....
* ....
* ....
* ....
* ....
* ....
* ....
* ....

Freundlichkeit der Woche:

Gesund gelebt?

	M	D	M	D	F	S	S

WOCHENPLANER

Montag

Dienstag

Mittwoch

Donnerstag

Freitag

Dringende To Dos:

*................................
*................................
*................................
*................................
*................................

Andere To Dos:

*................................
*................................
*................................
*................................
*................................
*................................
*................................
*................................
*................................
*................................
*................................
*................................
*................................
*................................
*................................

Freundlichkeit der Woche:

Gesund gelebt?

Gesund gelebt?	M	D	M	D	F	S	S

WOCHENPLANER

Woche:

Montag

Dienstag

Mittwoch

Donnerstag

Freitag

WEEKEND

Dringende To Dos:

* ____________________
* ____________________
* ____________________
* ____________________
* ____________________

Andere To Dos:

* ____________________
* ____________________
* ____________________
* ____________________
* ____________________
* ____________________
* ____________________
* ____________________
* ____________________
* ____________________
* ____________________
* ____________________
* ____________________
* ____________________

Freundlichkeit der Woche:

Gesund gelebt? M D M D F S S

WOCHENPLANER

Montag

Dienstag

Mittwoch

Donnerstag

Freitag

WEEKEND

Dringende To Dos:

* ....
* ....
* ....
* ....
* ....

Andere To Dos:

* ....
* ....
* ....
* ....
* ....
* ....
* ....
* ....
* ....
* ....
* ....
* ....
* ....
* ....

Freundlichkeit der Woche:

Gesund gelebt?   M D M D F S S

WOCHENPLANER

Montag

Dienstag

Mittwoch

Donnerstag

Freitag

Dringende To Dos:

*
*
*
*
*

Andere To Dos:

*
*
*
*
*
*
*
*
*
*
*
*
*
*
*

Freundlichkeit der Woche:

Gesund gelebt?	M	D	M	D	F	S	S

WOCHENPLANER

Montag

Dienstag

Mittwoch

Donnerstag

Freitag

Dringende To Dos:

* ....
* ....
* ....
* ....
* ....

Andere To-Dos:

* ....
* ....
* ....
* ....
* ....
* ....
* ....
* ....
* ....
* ....
* ....
* ....
* ....
* ....
* ....

Freundlichkeit der Woche:

Gesund gelebt?   M D M D F S S

WOCHENPLANER

Montag

Dienstag

Mittwoch

Donnerstag

Freitag

Dringende To Dos:

*
*
*
*
*

Andere To Dos:

*
*
*
*
*
*
*
*
*
*
*
*
*
*

Freundlichkeit der Woche:

Gesund gelebt? M D M D F S S

WOCHENPLANER

Woche:

Montag

Dienstag

Mittwoch

Donnerstag

Freitag

WEEKEND

Dringende To Dos:

*
*
*
*
*

Andere To-Dos:

*
*
*
*
*
*
*
*
*
*
*
*
*
*
*

Freundlichkeit der Woche:

Gesund gelebt?

	M	D	M	D	F	S	S

WOCHENPLANER

Montag

Dienstag

Mittwoch

Donnerstag

Freitag

Dringende To Dos:

*
*
*
*
*

Andere To Dos:

*
*
*
*
*
*
*
*
*
*
*
*
*
*
*

Freundlichkeit der Woche:

Gesund gelebt? M D M D F S S

WOCHENPLANER

Montag

Dienstag

Mittwoch

Donnerstag

Freitag

Dringende To Dos:

*
*
*
*
*

Andere To Dos:

*
*
*
*
*
*
*
*
*
*
*
*
*
*
*

Freundlichkeit der Woche:

Gesund gelebt?   M D M D F S S

WOCHENPLANER

Montag

Dienstag

Mittwoch

Donnerstag

Freitag

WEEKEND

Dringende To Dos:

*
*
*
*
*

Andere To Dos:

*
*
*
*
*
*
*
*
*
*
*
*
*
*
*

Freundlichkeit der Woche:

Gesund gelebt? M D M D F S S

WOCHENPLANER

Montag

Dienstag

Mittwoch

Donnerstag

Freitag

Dringende To Dos:

*
*
*
*
*

Andere To Dos:

*
*
*
*
*
*
*
*
*
*
*
*
*
*

Freundlichkeit der Woche:

Gesund gelebt?   M D M D F S S

WOCHENPLANER

Montag

Dienstag

Mittwoch

Donnerstag

Freitag

Dringende To Dos:

*
*
*
*
*

Andere To Dos:

*
*
*
*
*
*
*
*
*
*
*
*
*
*
*
*

Freundlichkeit der Woche:

Gesund gelebt? M D M D F S S

WOCHENPLANER

Montag

Dienstag

Mittwoch

Donnerstag

Freitag

Dringende To Dos:

*
*
*
*
*

Andere To Dos:

*
*
*
*
*
*
*
*
*
*
*
*
*
*

Freundlichkeit der Woche:

Gesund gelebt?	M	D	M	D	F	S	S

WOCHENPLANER

Woche:

Montag

Dienstag

Mittwoch

Donnerstag

Freitag

Dringende To Dos:

*
*
*
*
*

Andere To Dos:

*
*
*
*
*
*
*
*
*
*
*
*
*

Freundlichkeit der Woche:

Gesund gelebt?   M D M D F S S

WOCHENPLANER

Woche:

Montag

Dienstag

Mittwoch

Donnerstag

Freitag

WEEKEND

Dringende To Dos:

*
*
*
*
*

Andere To Dos:

*
*
*
*
*
*
*
*
*
*
*
*
*
*
*

Freundlichkeit der Woche:

Gesund gelebt? M D M D F S S

WOCHENPLANER

Woche:

Dringende To Dos:

*
*
*
*
*

Andere To Dos:

*
*
*
*
*
*
*
*
*
*
*
*
*

Freundlichkeit der Woche:

Gesund gelebt?	M	D	M	D	F	S	S

WOCHENPLANER

Montag

Dienstag

Mittwoch

Donnerstag

Freitag

WEEKEND

Dringende To Dos:

* ________________________
* ________________________
* ________________________
* ________________________
* ________________________

Andere To-Dos:

* ________________________
* ________________________
* ________________________
* ________________________
* ________________________
* ________________________
* ________________________
* ________________________
* ________________________
* ________________________
* ________________________
* ________________________
* ________________________
* ________________________

Freundlichkeit der Woche:

Gesund gelebt?	M	D	M	D	F	S	S

WOCHENPLANER

Montag

Dienstag

Mittwoch

Donnerstag

Freitag

Dringende To Dos:

* ....
* ....
* ....
* ....
* ....

Andere To Dos:

* ....
* ....
* ....
* ....
* ....
* ....
* ....
* ....
* ....
* ....
* ....
* ....
* ....
* ....
* ....

Freundlichkeit der Woche:

Gesund gelebt?	M	D	M	D	F	S	S

WOCHENPLANER

Woche:

Montag

Dienstag

Mittwoch

Donnerstag

Freitag

Dringende To Dos:

*
*
*
*
*

Andere To Dos:

*
*
*
*
*
*
*
*
*
*
*
*
*
*

Freundlichkeit der Woche:

Gesund gelebt?	M	D	M	D	F	S	S

WOCHENPLANER

Montag

Dienstag

Mittwoch

Donnerstag

Freitag

Dringende To Dos:

*
*
*
*
*

Andere To Dos:

*
*
*
*
*
*
*
*
*
*
*
*
*
*
*

Freundlichkeit der Woche:

Gesund gelebt?	M	D	M	D	F	S	S

WOCHENPLANER

Montag

Dienstag

Mittwoch

Donnerstag

Freitag

Dringende To Dos:

*
*
*
*
*

Andere To Dos:

*
*
*
*
*
*
*
*
*
*
*
*
*
*
*

Freundlichkeit der Woche:

Gesund gelebt?	M	D	M	D	F	S	S

WOCHENPLANER

Montag

Dienstag

Mittwoch

Donnerstag

Freitag

Dringende To Dos:

*
*
*
*
*

Andere To Dos:

*
*
*
*
*
*
*
*
*
*
*
*
*

Freundlichkeit der Woche:

Gesund gelebt?	M	D	M	D	F	S	S

WOCHENPLANER

Woche:

Montag

Dienstag

Mittwoch

Donnerstag

Freitag

WEEKEND

Dringende To Dos:

*
*
*
*
*

Andere To Dos:

*
*
*
*
*
*
*
*
*
*
*
*
*
*

Freundlichkeit der Woche:

Gesund gelebt?	M	D	M	D	F	S	S

WOCHENPLANER

Woche:

Montag

Dienstag

Mittwoch

Donnerstag

Freitag

WEEKEND

Dringende To Dos:

*
*
*
*
*

Andere To Dos:

*
*
*
*
*
*
*
*
*
*
*
*
*
*
*

Freundlichkeit der Woche:

Gesund gelebt?

Gesund gelebt?	M	D	M	D	F	S	S

WOCHENPLANER

Woche:

Montag

Dienstag

Mittwoch

Donnerstag

Freitag

WEEKEND

Dringende To-Dos:

*
*
*
*
*

Andere To-Dos:

*
*
*
*
*
*
*
*
*
*
*
*
*
*

Freundlichkeit der Woche:

Gesund gelebt?

	M	D	M	D	F	S	S

WOCHENPLANER

Montag

Dienstag

Mittwoch

Donnerstag

Freitag

Dringende To Dos:

* ------------------------------
* ------------------------------
* ------------------------------
* ------------------------------
* ------------------------------

Andere To Dos:

* ------------------------------
* ------------------------------
* ------------------------------
* ------------------------------
* ------------------------------
* ------------------------------
* ------------------------------
* ------------------------------
* ------------------------------
* ------------------------------
* ------------------------------
* ------------------------------
* ------------------------------
* ------------------------------

Freundlichkeit der Woche:

Gesund gelebt? M D M D F S S

WOCHENPLANER

Montag

Dienstag

Mittwoch

Donnerstag

Freitag

Dringende To Dos:

*
*
*
*
*

Andere To Dos:

*
*
*
*
*
*
*
*
*
*
*
*
*
*

Freundlichkeit der Woche:

Gesund gelebt?	M	D	M	D	F	S	S

WOCHENPLANER

Montag

Dienstag

Mittwoch

Donnerstag

Freitag

Dringende To Dos:

*
*
*
*
*

Andere To Dos:

*
*
*
*
*
*
*
*
*
*
*
*
*
*
*

Freundlichkeit der Woche:

Gesund gelebt?

	M	D	M	D	F	S	S

WOCHENPLANER

Montag

Dienstag

Mittwoch

Donnerstag

Freitag

Dringende To Dos:

*
*
*
*
*

Andere To Dos:

*
*
*
*
*
*
*
*
*
*
*
*
*
*
*

Freundlichkeit der Woche:

Gesund gelebt? M D M D F S S

WOCHENPLANER

Montag

Dienstag

Mittwoch

Donnerstag

Freitag

Dringende To Dos:

*
*
*
*
*

Andere To Dos:

*
*
*
*
*
*
*
*
*
*
*
*
*
*

Freundlichkeit der Woche:

Gesund gelebt?	M	D	M	D	F	S	S

WOCHENPLANER

Montag

Dienstag

Mittwoch

Donnerstag

Freitag

Dringende To Dos:

*
*
*
*
*

Andere To Dos:

*
*
*
*
*
*
*
*
*
*
*
*
*
*
*
*

Freundlichkeit der Woche:

Gesund gelebt?

Gesund gelebt?	M	D	M	D	F	S	S

WOCHENPLANER

Woche:

Montag

Dienstag

Mittwoch

Donnerstag

Freitag

Dringende To Dos:

* ______________________
* ______________________
* ______________________
* ______________________
* ______________________

Andere To Dos:

* ______________________
* ______________________
* ______________________
* ______________________
* ______________________
* ______________________
* ______________________
* ______________________
* ______________________
* ______________________
* ______________________
* ______________________
* ______________________
* ______________________
* ______________________

Freundlichkeit der Woche:

Gesund gelebt? M D M D F S S

WOCHENPLANER

Woche:

Montag

Dienstag

Mittwoch

Donnerstag

Freitag

WEEKEND

Dringende To Dos:

* ____________________________________
* ____________________________________
* ____________________________________
* ____________________________________
* ____________________________________

Andere To Dos:

* ____________________________________
* ____________________________________
* ____________________________________
* ____________________________________
* ____________________________________
* ____________________________________
* ____________________________________
* ____________________________________
* ____________________________________
* ____________________________________
* ____________________________________
* ____________________________________
* ____________________________________
* ____________________________________
* ____________________________________

Freundlichkeit der Woche:

Gesund gelebt? M D M D F S S

WOCHENPLANER

Woche:

Montag

Dienstag

Mittwoch

Donnerstag

Freitag

Dringende To Dos:

*
*
*
*
*

Andere To Dos:

*
*
*
*
*
*
*
*
*
*
*
*
*
*

Freundlichkeit der Woche:

Gesund gelebt?

	M	D	M	D	F	S	S

WOCHENPLANER

Montag

Dienstag

Mittwoch

Donnerstag

Freitag

WEEKEND

Dringende To Dos:
*
*
*
*
*

Andere To Dos:
*
*
*
*
*
*
*
*
*
*
*
*
*
*
*

Freundlichkeit der Woche:

Gesund gelebt? M D M D F S S

WOCHENPLANER

Montag

Dienstag

Mittwoch

Donnerstag

Freitag

Dringende To Dos:

*
*
*
*
*

Andere To Dos:

*
*
*
*
*
*
*
*
*
*
*
*
*
*

Freundlichkeit der Woche:

Gesund gelebt? M D M D F S S

WOCHENPLANER

Woche:

Montag

Dienstag

Mittwoch

Donnerstag

Freitag

WEEKEND

Dringende To Dos:

*
*
*
*
*

Andere To-Dos:

*
*
*
*
*
*
*
*
*
*
*
*
*
*

Freundlichkeit der Woche:

Gesund gelebt?

	M	D	M	D	F	S	S

WOCHENPLANER

Montag

Dienstag

Mittwoch

Donnerstag

Freitag

WEEKEND

Dringende To Dos:

*
*
*
*
*

Andere To Dos:

*
*
*
*
*
*
*
*
*
*
*
*
*
*

Freundlichkeit der Woche:

Gesund gelebt? M D M D F S S

WOCHENPLANER

Woche:

Montag

Dienstag

Mittwoch

Donnerstag

Freitag

WEEKEND

Dringende To Dos:

*
*
*
*
*

Andere To Dos:

*
*
*
*
*
*
*
*
*
*
*
*
*
*
*

Freundlichkeit der Woche:

Gesund gelebt?	M	D	M	D	F	S	S

WOCHENPLANER

Montag

Dienstag

Mittwoch

Donnerstag

Freitag

Dringende To Dos:

*
*
*
*
*

Andere To Dos:

*
*
*
*
*
*
*
*
*
*
*
*
*
*
*

Freundlichkeit der Woche:

Gesund gelebt?

	M	D	M	D	F	S	S

WOCHENPLANER

Montag

Dienstag

Mittwoch

Donnerstag

Freitag

Dringende To Dos:

*
*
*
*
*

Andere To Dos:

*
*
*
*
*
*
*
*
*
*
*
*
*
*
*
*

Freundlichkeit der Woche:

Gesund gelebt? M D M D F S S

WOCHENPLANER

Montag

Dienstag

Mittwoch

Donnerstag

Freitag

Dringende To Dos:

* ....
* ....
* ....
* ....
* ....

Andere To Dos:

* ....
* ....
* ....
* ....
* ....
* ....
* ....
* ....
* ....
* ....
* ....
* ....
* ....
* ....
* ....

Freundlichkeit der Woche:

Gesund gelebt?

	M	D	M	D	F	S	S

WOCHENPLANER

Montag

Dienstag

Mittwoch

Donnerstag

Freitag

Dringende To Dos:

* _______________________
* _______________________
* _______________________
* _______________________
* _______________________

Andere To Dos:

* _______________________
* _______________________
* _______________________
* _______________________
* _______________________
* _______________________
* _______________________
* _______________________
* _______________________
* _______________________
* _______________________
* _______________________
* _______________________
* _______________________

Freundlichkeit der Woche:

Gesund gelebt?

	M	D	M	D	F	S	S

WOCHENPLANER

Montag

Dienstag

Mittwoch

Donnerstag

Freitag

Dringende To Dos:

*
*
*
*
*

Andere To Dos:

*
*
*
*
*
*
*
*
*
*
*
*
*
*

Freundlichkeit der Woche:

Gesund gelebt? M D M D F S S

WOCHENPLANER

Montag

Dienstag

Mittwoch

Donnerstag

Freitag

Dringende To Dos:

*
*
*
*
*

Andere To Dos:

*
*
*
*
*
*
*
*
*
*
*
*
*
*
*

Freundlichkeit der Woche:

Gesund gelebt?	M	D	M	D	F	S	S

WOCHENPLANER

Montag

Dienstag

Mittwoch

Donnerstag

Freitag

Dringende To Dos:

*
*
*
*
*

Andere To Dos:

*
*
*
*
*
*
*
*
*
*
*
*
*
*
*

Freundlichkeit der Woche:

Gesund gelebt? M D M D F S S

WOCHENPLANER

Dringende To Dos:

*
*
*
*
*

Andere To Dos:

*
*
*
*
*
*
*
*
*
*
*
*
*
*

Freundlichkeit der Woche:

Montag

Dienstag

Mittwoch

Donnerstag

Freitag

Gesund gelebt?	M	D	M	D	F	S	S

WOCHENPLANER

Woche:

Montag

Dienstag

Mittwoch

Donnerstag

Freitag

WEEKEND

Dringende To Dos:

*
*
*
*
*

Andere To Dos:

*
*
*
*
*
*
*
*
*
*
*
*
*
*

Freundlichkeit der Woche:

Gesund gelebt?	M	D	M	D	F	S	S

WOCHENPLANER

Montag

Dienstag

Mittwoch

Donnerstag

Freitag

Dringende To Dos:

*
*
*
*
*

Andere To Dos:

*
*
*
*
*
*
*
*
*
*
*
*
*
*

Freundlichkeit der Woche:

Gesund gelebt?   M D M D F S S

WOCHENPLANER

Montag

Dienstag

Mittwoch

Donnerstag

Freitag

Dringende To Dos:

* ____________________
* ____________________
* ____________________
* ____________________
* ____________________

Andere To Dos:

* ____________________
* ____________________
* ____________________
* ____________________
* ____________________
* ____________________
* ____________________
* ____________________
* ____________________
* ____________________
* ____________________
* ____________________
* ____________________
* ____________________

Freundlichkeit der Woche:

Gesund gelebt?

	M	D	M	D	F	S	S

WOCHENPLANER

Montag

Dienstag

Mittwoch

Donnerstag

Freitag

WEEKEND

Dringende To Dos:

* ______________________________
* ______________________________
* ______________________________
* ______________________________
* ______________________________

Andere To Dos:

* ______________________________
* ______________________________
* ______________________________
* ______________________________
* ______________________________
* ______________________________
* ______________________________
* ______________________________
* ______________________________
* ______________________________
* ______________________________
* ______________________________
* ______________________________
* ______________________________
* ______________________________
* ______________________________

Freundlichkeit der Woche:

Gesund gelebt?

	M	D	M	D	F	S	S

WOCHENPLANER

Montag

Dienstag

Mittwoch

Donnerstag

Freitag

Dringende To Dos:

*
*
*
*
*

Andere To Dos:

*
*
*
*
*
*
*
*
*
*
*
*
*
*

Freundlichkeit der Woche:

Gesund gelebt?

	M	D	M	D	F	S	S

WOCHENPLANER

Montag

Dienstag

Mittwoch

Donnerstag

Freitag

WEEKEND

Dringende To-Dos:

*
*
*
*
*

Andere To-Dos:

*
*
*
*
*
*
*
*
*
*
*
*
*
*
*

Freundlichkeit der Woche:

Gesund gelebt?	M	D	M	D	F	S	S

WOCHENPLANER

Woche:

Montag

Dienstag

Mittwoch

Donnerstag

Freitag

WEEKEND

Dringende To Dos:

*
*
*
*
*

Andere To Dos:

*
*
*
*
*
*
*
*
*
*
*
*
*
*
*

Freundlichkeit der Woche:

Gesund gelebt?

	M	D	M	D	F	S	S

WOCHENPLANER

Montag

Dienstag

Mittwoch

Donnerstag

Freitag

Dringende To Dos:

*
*
*
*
*

Andere To Dos:

*
*
*
*
*
*
*
*
*
*
*
*
*
*
*
*

Freundlichkeit der Woche:

Gesund gelebt?

	M	D	M	D	F	S	S

WOCHENPLANER

Montag

Dienstag

Mittwoch

Donnerstag

Freitag

Dringende To Dos:

*
*
*
*
*

Andere To Dos:

*
*
*
*
*
*
*
*
*
*
*
*
*
*

Freundlichkeit der Woche:

Gesund gelebt?   M D M D F S S

	M	D	M	D	F	S	S

WOCHENPLANER

Montag

Dienstag

Mittwoch

Donnerstag

Freitag

Dringende To Dos:

*
*
*
*
*

Andere To Dos:

*
*
*
*
*
*
*
*
*
*
*
*
*
*

Freundlichkeit der Woche:

Gesund gelebt?

	M	D	M	D	F	S	S

WOCHENPLANER

Montag

Dienstag

Mittwoch

Donnerstag

Freitag

Dringende To Dos:

*
*
*
*
*

Andere To Dos:

*
*
*
*
*
*
*
*
*
*
*
*
*
*

Freundlichkeit der Woche:

Gesund gelebt?

	M	D	M	D	F	S	S

WOCHENPLANER

Montag

Dienstag

Mittwoch

Donnerstag

Freitag

Dringende To-Dos:

*
*
*
*
*

Andere To-Dos:

*
*
*
*
*
*
*
*
*
*
*
*
*
*

Freundlichkeit der Woche:

Gesund gelebt?	M	D	M	D	F	S	S

WOCHENPLANER

Montag

Dienstag

Mittwoch

Donnerstag

Freitag

Dringende To Dos:

* ....
* ....
* ....
* ....
* ....

Andere To Dos:

* ....
* ....
* ....
* ....
* ....
* ....
* ....
* ....
* ....
* ....
* ....
* ....
* ....
* ....

Freundlichkeit der Woche:

Gesund gelebt? M D M D F S S

WOCHENPLANER

Montag

Dienstag

Mittwoch

Donnerstag

Freitag

Dringende To Dos:

*
*
*
*
*

Andere To Dos:

*
*
*
*
*
*
*
*
*
*
*
*
*
*

Freundlichkeit der Woche:

Gesund gelebt?

	M	D	M	D	F	S	S

WOCHENPLANER

Woche:

Montag

Dienstag

Mittwoch

Donnerstag

Freitag

WEEKEND

Dringende To Dos:

* ....
* ....
* ....
* ....
* ....

Andere To Dos:

* ....
* ....
* ....
* ....
* ....
* ....
* ....
* ....
* ....
* ....
* ....
* ....
* ....
* ....

Freundlichkeit der Woche:

Gesund gelebt?   M D M D F S S